D0378960

© 2003 by Barbour Publishing, Inc.

ISBN 1-58660-877-0

All rights reserved. No part of this publication may be reproduced or transmitted in any form or by any means without written permission of the publisher.

Cover image © Creatas

Scripture quotations are taken from the King James Version of the Bible.

Published by Barbour Publishing, Inc., P.O. Box 719, Uhrichsville, Ohio 44683, www.barbourbooks.com

Member of the
Evangelical Christian
Publishers Association

Printed in China.

5 4 3 2 1

Come to the Manger

MARILOU H. FLINKMAN

If holidays bring out visions of Santa Claus,

twinkling lights,

and reindeer with red noses,

you need to change your view.

Think Holy-days

and remember the first Christmas.

It all started with a manger.

I invite you to join me as we follow the path to the manger.

Let's start by going back to the prophets of old.

They will tell us where to start our journey.

For unto us a child is born, unto us a son is given:

and the government shall be upon his shoulder:

and his name shall be called Wonderful,

Counsellor,

The mighty God,

The everlasting Father,

The Prince of Peace.

ISAIAH 9:6

Those ancient words bring hope to the world. How would we react if we saw those words as the headline in the morning paper? Would we scoff or would we fall on our knees in thanksgiving?

Would we turn to the rest of the story on the back pages to see where this miracle man could be found? Or would we use the paper to line the birdcage?

Read Isaiah's words again and decide if you will set your course for the North Pole or will you join me to search for the Prince of Peace.

 $\mathscr{I}$ invite you to believe that the Prince of Peace is at hand. Together we can follow the path to find this wonderful counselor, this mighty God who will shoulder the government. We won't find Him in a palace nor will He be in a big government office. We will find the everlasting Father in a manger. Come, let us search for that manger.

And it shall be said in that day,

Lo, this is our God;

we have waited for him,

and he will save us: this is the LORD;

we have waited for him,

we will be glad and rejoice in his salvation.

ISAIAH 25:9

He has come to save mankind. But in this world of wars, famine, and strife, where will we find Him? Isaiah's words are centuries old. Are we too late to find the Savior? Has He come and found us too sinful to save?

We are told to come to the manger. Where will we find this place? Will it be the same for all of us? Follow the prophets for a clue to the answers.

But thou, Bethlehem Ephratah, though thou

be little among the thousands of Judah,

yet out of thee shall he come forth unto me that is to be ruler in Israel;

whose goings forth have been from of old, from everlasting.

MICAH 5:2

We can take hope from the words of Micah. He tells us the one who comes to rule Israel is from the everlasting. If this was true in Micah's time, won't we still find the promised Holy One of God? Won't we find the manger?

Come to the Manger

Come Thou long expected Jesus,

Born to set Thy people free;

From our fears and sins release us;

Let us find our rest in Thee.

Israel's strength and consolation,

Hope of all the earth Thou art;

Dear desire of every nation,

Joy of every longing heart.

Born Thy people to deliver,

Born a child, and yet a King,

Born to reign in us for ever,

Now Thy gracious kingdom bring.

By Thine own eternal Spirit,

Rule in all our hearts alone;

By Thine all-sufficient merit,

Raise us to Thy glorious throne.

OLD ENGLISH HYMN

And in the sixth month the angel Gabriel was sent from God

unto a city of Galilee, named Nazareth. . . .

And the angel said unto her, Fear not, Mary:

for thou hast found favour with God.

And, behold, thou shalt conceive in thy womb,

and bring forth a son, and shalt call his name JESUS.

He shall be great, and shall be called the Son of the Highest:

and the Lord God shall give unto him the throne of his father David:

And he shall reign over the house of Jacob for ever;

and of his kingdom there shall be no end.

LUKE 1:26, 30–33

The young teen Mary listened to the angel who explained how these things would be possible. The daily routine of her life would be turned upside down and thrown into confusion. Yet with great faith she faced the unknown and said, "yes."

And Mary said,

Behold the handmaid of the Lord;

be it unto me according to thy word.

And the angel departed from her.

LUKE 1:38

The angel sped on wings of light,

    With wondrous tidings laden;

He came from heav'ns unclouded height,

    To greet a lowly maiden.

For God upon her low estate

    Had looked with royal favour:

And all earth's kindreds celebrate

    The mighty Gift He gave her.

O awful bliss! That from her womb

    Should spring the Uncreated,

The great and holy One, for whom

    The world so long had waited.

OLD ENGLISH HYMN

Then Joseph her husband, being a just man,

and not willing to make her a public example,

was minded to put her away privily.

But while he thought on these things,

behold, the angel of the LORD appeared

unto him in a dream, saying,

Joseph, thou son of David,

fear not to take unto thee Mary thy wife:

for that which is conceived in her is of the Holy Ghost.

And she shall bring forth a son,

and thou shalt call his name JESUS:

for he shall save his people from their sins.

MATTHEW 1:19–21

Joseph expected life to take a predictable course—a wedding, a family, and the daily life of a carpenter. When Mary came to him with her story, he was ready to quietly bow out. Then an angel came to him with the message that overcame human logic. Could this be true? Could this young girl to whom he was betrothed actually bring forth the Son of God?

The beauty of Mary and Joseph's faith sets the example for us. We must continue on the path to find a world of peace. We must seek justice and love. We must seek the Christ Child.

And Mary arose in those days,

and went into the hill country with haste,

into a city of Juda;

And entered into the house of Zacharias,

and saluted Elisabeth.

And it came to pass, that,

when Elisabeth heard the salutation of Mary,

the babe leaped in her womb;

and Elisabeth was filled with the Holy Ghost:

And she spake out with a loud voice, and said,

Blessed art thou among women,

and blessed is the fruit of thy womb.

And whence is this to me,

that the mother of my Lord should come to me?

LUKE 1:39–43

*C*an't you see a young confused girl running to a favorite relative to be consoled? When Mary came to her cousin and Elisabeth greeted her with joy, she must have felt comfort. Elisabeth recognized Mary's condition and the details of how it came to be. Mary could relax in the knowledge that Elisabeth, whom she loved and trusted, understood her story.

Here Mary offers her prayer for her people, for the consolation of Israel. Do you think she knew how deeply her people's yearning would take root in her? Could she see the future and know what part God would open to her?

We don't know where our path will lead, but this girl's faith is an example for us to follow.

THE SONG OF MARY

My soul proclaims the greatness of the Lord,

my spirit rejoices in God my Savior:

for he has looked with favor on his lowly servant.

From this day all generations will call me blessed:

The Almighty has done great things for me,

And holy is his Name.

He has mercy on those who fear him in every generation.

He has shown the strength of his arm,

He has scattered the proud in their conceit.

He has cast down the mighty from their

thrones, and has lifted up the lowly.

He has filled the hungry with good things,

And the rich he has sent away empty.

He has come to the help of his servant Israel,

for he has remembered his promise of mercy, the

promise he made to our fathers, to Abraham

and his children for ever.

LUKE 1:46–55 (PARAPHRASED)

Historians tell us Mary was about fourteen to fifteen years old. Can you believe those words came from a child of that age? We have to believe she was touched by God.

Her yearnings, voiced in the Magnificat, echo our own feelings today. Don't we long to bring the hungry, the naked, the diseased before God that they may feel His compassion? Aren't we drawn to care for His people? It is His strength that fills us with the courage to stay on the path, to find our way to the Christ Child who will save the world.

And Mary abode with her about three months,
and returned to her own house.

LUKE 1:56

Mary had to return to the world she grew up in. Nazareth must have buzzed with gossip. The quick trip to visit her cousin and sudden marriage to Joseph would have set tongues wagging. But we have seen the strength of this young woman. She is no ordinary bride. She is preparing herself to care for the Son of God. She is following the path God has set before her.

Of the Father's love begotten,

Ere the worlds began to be,

He the Alpha and Omega,

He the source, the ending He,

Of the things that are, that have been,

And that future years shall see,

Evermore and evermore!

Christ, to Thee with God the Father,

And, O Holy Ghost, to Thee,

Hymn and chant and high thanksgiving

And unwearied praises be:

Honour, glory, and dominion,

And eternal victory,

Evermore and evermore!

OLD ENGLISH HYMN

And it came to pass in those days,

that there went out a decree from Caesar Augustus

that all the world should be taxed.

(And this taxing was first made when Cyrenius was governor of Syria.)

And all went to be taxed, every one into his own city.

LUKE 2:1–3

GOD EVEN USES THE TAXMAN!

THE CHRIST CHILD

WAS TO BE BORN IN BETHLEHEM,

AND THIS IS HOW THE LORD

BROUGHT MARY TO THE PLACE SPOKEN OF IN THE PROPHETS.

And Joseph also went up from Galilee,

out of the city of Nazareth,

into Judaea, unto the city of David,

which is called Bethlehem;

(because he was of the house and lineage of David:)

to be taxed with Mary his espoused wife,

being great with child.

LUKE 2:4–5

Nine months pregnant and riding a donkey from Nazareth to Bethlehem shows this girl's courage. Could our path be any harder? Can we stop now on our goal to find the manger?

And so it was, that, while they were there,

the days were accomplished that she should be delivered.

And she brought forth her firstborn son,

and wrapped him in swaddling clothes,

and laid him in a manger;

because there was no room for them in the inn.

LUKE 2:6–7

There was no sterile hospital, not even a midwife.

The Son of God was born in a stable. His humble bed a

manger, the very manger we seek today. How will we

find our way? *Faith will be our guide.*

And there were in the same country shepherds abiding in the field, keeping watch over their flock by night.

And, lo, the angel of the Lord came upon them, and the glory of the Lord shone round about them: and they were sore afraid.

And the angel said unto them, Fear not: for, behold, I bring you good tidings of great joy, which shall be to all people.

For unto you is born this day in the city of David a Saviour, which is Christ the Lord.

And this shall be a sign unto you; Ye shall find the babe wrapped in swaddling clothes, lying in a manger.

And suddenly there was with the angel a multitude of the heavenly host praising God, and saying,

Glory to God in the highest, and on earth peace, good will toward men.

Luke 2:8–14

Hark! The herald angels sing,
　　"Glory to the newborn King:
Peace on earth and mercy mild,
　　God and sinners reconciled!"
Joyful, all ye nations rise,
　　Join the triumph of the skies;
With angelic host proclaim,
　　"Christ is born in Bethlehem!"

Hail the heaven-born Prince of Peace!
　　Hail the Son of Righteousness!
Light and life to all He brings,
　　Risen with healing in His wings,
Mild He lays His glory by,
　　Born that man no more may die,
Born to raise the sons of earth,
　　Born to give them second birth.
Hark the herald angels sing,
　　"Glory to the newborn King."

CHARLES WESLEY

27

Come to the Manger

The first to worship at the manger were shepherds from the fields. The angels of heaven guided them to the Christ Child. These were simple workingmen who probably could not read. We have the prophets of old and the Scriptures of the Gospels to guide us. They followed the star of Bethlehem to the stable. We will follow the light that still shines in the world if we will but look for it.

Don't be led astray by the tinsel and flickering lights of the secular world around us. Seek the radiance of God's glory. We can only miss it if we aren't looking.

And it came to pass,
as the angels were gone away from them into heaven,
the shepherds said one to another,
Let us now go even unto Bethlehem,
and see this thing which is come to pass,
which the Lord hath made known unto us.
And they came with haste, and found Mary, and Joseph,
and the babe lying in a manger.

Luke 2:15–16

28

Why would God call you or me?

Why should we believe He will guide us to the manger?

If we have faith, we know that God made us.

We are His from the moment of birth.

He will lead us to place of His Son's

birth—even to a smelly sheep pen.

Are we looking for the manger in the wrong place?
The shepherds found the Christ Child lying in a sheep
pen with only Mary, Joseph, and animals around Him.

We knew at the start of our search we would
not find the manger in a palace or an important office.
We must seek the humble abode of all God's people.
Some may live in a grand home and find the Lord will
dwell with them there. More of us will find our Master's
manger in the most humble place we can think of.
The innkeeper would never believe he sent the Son of
God to sleep in the barn. Will we miss our chance to
worship at the manger simply because we are not looking?

Come to the Manger

And when they had seen it, they made known abroad the saying which was told them concerning this child. And all they that heard it wondered at those things which were told them by the shepherds.

LUKE 2:17–18

How would people react today if they were told the Messiah lay in the arms of a teenager on the outskirts of their village? Would they be part of the group who scoffed at the story and went on with their busy lives?

Be open to the message.

Be ready to believe when you hear God calling.

Who is this child in the manger? COULD IT BE THE SON OF GOD WOULD COME INTO THE WORLD NOT ONLY AS A NEWBORN BABY BUT CONSENT TO BE BORN IN A BARN? HE LIES WRAPPED IN STRIPS OF CLOTH HIS MOTHER BROUGHT WITH HER. THE STAR OVER THE STABLE STILL SHINES, BUT THE ANGELS ARE GONE. HUMBLE SHEPHERDS KNEEL BY THE MANGER IN AWE OF WHAT THEY SEE THERE.

Now when Jesus was born in Bethlehem of Judaea

in the days of Herod the king, behold,

there came wise men from the east to Jerusalem, saying,

Where is he that is born King of the Jews?

for we have seen his star in the east,

and are come to worship him.

MATTHEW 2:1–2

31

The wise men followed the star and found Jesus lying in a manger. The smelly sheep pen did not stop them. They fell on their knees and worshiped the Christ Child. They gave Him gifts of gold, frankincense, and myrrh.

Brightest and best of the sons of the morning,
Dawn on our darkness and lend us thine aid:
Star of the East, the horizon adorning,
Guide where our infant Redeemer is laid.
Vainly we offer each ample oblation,
Vainly with gifts would His favour secure:
Richer by far is the heart's adoration,
Dearer to God are the prayers of the poor.

OLD ENGLISH HYMN

And being warned of God in a dream that they

should not return to Herod, they departed into

their own country another way.

MATTHEW 2:12

Will we be like these wise men of old?
Will we jump out of the rat race to
celebrate Christmas with prayer and
gifts to others? When the glitter of the
celebration is past, will we follow the
words of Christ and go on with life
on the Christian path?

The wise men turned away
from the evil they saw in Herod.
Let's take a lesson from them and
avoid the lure of the world. Let's
look for the manger and the blessing
waiting there for us.

And when eight days were accomplished

for the circumcising of the child, his name

was called *JESUS*, which was so named of

the angel before he was conceived in the womb.

And when the days of her purification according

to the law of Moses were accomplished, they

brought him to Jerusalem, to present

him to the Lord.

LUKE 2:21–22

Joseph and Mary obeyed the laws of Moses.

They brought the baby for circumcision and called

His name Jesus. The name was not uncommon,

being a later form of the Hebrew

name Joshua, meaning savior.

And, behold,

there was a man in Jerusalem, whose name was Simeon;

and the same man was just and devout,

waiting for the consolation of Israel:

and the Holy Ghost was upon him.

And it was revealed unto him by the Holy Ghost, that

he should not see death, before he had seen the Lord's Christ.

And he came by the Spirit into the temple: and when

the parents brought in the child Jesus,

to do for him after the custom of the law,

then took he him up in his arms, and blessed God, and said,

Lord, now lettest thou thy servant depart in peace,

according to thy word.

For mine eyes have seen thy salvation,

which thou hast prepared before the face of all people;

a light to lighten the Gentiles,

and the glory of thy people Israel.

LUKE 2:25–32

*L*ed by the Holy Spirit,

Simeon waited in the temple

when Jesus was presented by His parents.

We will be led to the manger where

Christ waits if we are just

willing to follow the Spirit.

And there was one Anna, a prophetess. . .

And she was a widow of about fourscore and four years, which departed not from the temple, but served God with fastings and prayers night and day.

And she coming in that instant gave thanks likewise unto the Lord, and spake of him to all them that looked for redemption in Jerusalem.

Luke 2:36–38

ANNA AND SIMEON WERE CALLED INTO THE TEMPLE

TO RECEIVE THE CHRIST CHILD.

Where will we be?

We have followed the path.

Our manger is waiting.

Whether it is in a church,

the company of laughing children

and loved ones, or in the silence

of a hospital room,

or a lonely apartment.

You only have to close your eyes and

open your heart and come to the manger.

Jesus Christ is waiting for you.

Glory to God in the highest,

and peace to His people on earth.